TOBOGGAN RUN

A Collection of Short Stories

By: Scott Keenan

D1518272

SCOTT KEENAN

TOBOGGAN RUN

A Collection of Short Stories

BY SCOTT KEENAN

Published by: Scott Keenan Books
Copyright © May 2024, Scott Keenan Consulting, LLC
All rights reserved.

SCOTT KEENAN BOOKS
http://scottkeenanbooks.com

Paperback ISBN: 9798326012937

Cover artwork, book layout, and formatting by:
Angie Simonson, Main Idea Creative

Printed in the United States of America

SCOTT KEENAN

Thank you, Louie St. George III, for providing your excellent editing skills to make Toboggan Run a reality. The book would never have been possible without you.

Louie St. George III is a former journalist who wrote about sports for the Duluth News Tribune (Minnesota) and Farmington Daily Times (New Mexico). He works in public relations in Duluth, where he lives with his family, and is a freelance writer and editor. St. George is also an aspiring middle-of-the-pack runner who frequently can be found training on Duluth's roads or trails for his next marathon.

TOBOGGAN RUN

A Collection of Short Stories

By: Scott Keenan

scottkeenanbooks.com

Table of Contents

INTRODUCTION...11

Chapter 1 THE OLD FARMER...........................13

Chapter 2 CHRISTMAS WALNUTS 17

Chapter 3 TOBOGGAN RUN 21

Chapter 4 THE HIDDEN VALLEY.......................25

Chapter 5 RUNNING A BUSINESS....................28

Chapter 6 THE SECRET SPRING 32

Chapter 7 CLIFF ROCK 35

Chapter 8 FAIRMONT PARK 38

Chapter 9 RUSTY THE TOM CAT......................41

Chapter 10 THE ELUSIVE HAZELNUTS 44

Chapter 11 SATURDAY NIGHT BATH 46

Chapter 12 NIGHT SKIING 49

Chapter 13 ARROWS IN THE SKY 52

Chapter 14 WINTER STORMS...........................55

Chapter 15 THE MILKY WAY.............................59

Chapter 16 AGATE HUNTING 62

Chapter 17 THE NEXT-DOOR NEIGHBOR 66

Chapter 18 UNCLE UNO 70

Chapter 19 CATHOLIC CHURCH 74

Chapter 20 READY OR NOT, HERE I COME......77

Chapter 21 GO-KART RACING 80

Chapter 22 MOTHER GOES FISHING 83

Chapter 23 THE GREEN BUMBOAT 86

Chapter 24 HE'S SAFE..91

Chapter 25 THE NEIGHBORHOOD...................95

IN CLOSING 99

ABOUT THE AUTHOR 101

*This collection of short stories is
solely based on my memories as a child.*

INTRODUCTION

I am sure most people, as they grow older, have some childhood memories deeply rooted in the back of their cerebrum. I am no different, and as I am now in my seventh decade of life, I find those recollections appearing more often. They are occurring in my nightly dreams or when I am working in the backyard gardens. Most of them are good memories.

I am not positive that any of these past experiences of mine are book-worthy, but that wasn't a factor in why I started to write my collection of short stories. I felt it was important to put the pen to the paper, so I did. It gave me some peace and serenity, and more importantly it was a small tribute to honor some of my close childhood friends.

Time quickly goes by in life and I have lost so many of my dear friends to horrific diseases. I often wonder why I am still alive, walking and breathing on this third planet from the sun. I never emerge from that thought process with any answers. It is hard for me not to shed a tear when I am thinking spiritually of them.

This book was a very enjoyable journey to take. I hope if nothing else you can feel the magic of this one child during his early stages of adolescence in the 1960s, and maybe it will help you to rekindle your special childhood memories.

This book is dedicated to all who care for and love those special friends.

Scott Keenan

Chapter 1
THE OLD FARMER

The field was covered with tall prairie grass that was hiding the view of the old well, overlaid with just a few dilapidated boards. No one knew exactly its location, but it was somewhere near the edge of the old chicken farm's property line. The well was rumored to be 30 or 40 feet deep and provided the necessary water for the farm needs. The windows of the largest of the two barns were all broken and the walls were sagging inwards. The harsh Minnesota winters had taken their toll. The pine boards were heavily weathered and only appealing to a few collectors of the cherished barn wood.

The old farmer would first appear in late spring after the snow was melted and the rich soil had warmed and softened. He had two large garden plots, one located only yards from the nearest building. The second was 100 yards or so to the north, just past the old majestic oak tree. The land was hand-tilled by primitive tools; there was no desire from the farmer to use modern equipment to ease his chores.

No one knew the farmer's name. He seemed to work all day in the warm sun with his wide-brim straw hat protecting his already chiseled face. He drove his old Ford pickup truck, aged by time, the dark green paint well faded with rust embossed in most of its body. The road to the farmer's property was overgrown and crossed a wobbling wooden-covered log bridge between two small swamps leading to his land's edge.

All we knew of the farmer was he seemed so old. We never spoke to him, nor did he make any effort to speak to us. We were not afraid of him, but curious about who he was.

My older brother, myself and our neighborhood friends cherished the fall harvest days, as the many crops were ripened for picking. We may have been a little reckless and daring, but we carefully planned our raid for one late-fall afternoon. The carrots, onions, corn and potatoes were planted in carefully groomed rows. We flawlessly executed our plan on the carrot row and quickly pulled a dozen or so from the well-tilled soil. We took what we could eat and disappeared into the nearby woods.

The old oak tree near one of the garden plots, sublime in nature with its many large limbs protruding from its crown, came under attack one summer day, from all of us in the neighborhood. Old boards and rusty nails were salvaged from the chicken coops, hammers and saws were borrowed without permission from my dad's work shed. Wooden steps were pounded deep into the core of the tree so we could ascend to the largest branches extending outwards 30 feet above the ground. Boards were hoisted by old frayed Manila hemp ropes and within days our platform was finished. No walls, just the base where we could hang out and be alone telling stories and sharing dreams. The farmer didn't seem to care. No words were ever exchanged.

Chapter 2
CHRISTMAS WALNUTS

Christmas season in the 1950s and early '60s was a special time for me as I was growing up in Duluth's Kenwood neighborhood. There was no extra money for presents, but mom and dad always made the holidays feel special for their four children.

We were probably considered a poor family, but we never knew it and never felt it. We were always busy enjoying our youth and

17

staying active outside. We never seemed to spend much time indoors.

I learned at a very young age that if you wanted extra special possessions you had to buy them yourself.

I started earning my own money at the age of 9 with my newspaper route. I also delivered groceries to the elderly in close proximity to my home, and mowed as many lawns as I could! I was obsessed with making money, and I was considered by many to be a little frugal and a very good saver.

Like any child, the excitement of the approaching holiday was flowing through my veins. It wasn't only about receiving presents; it was more about enjoying the activities leading up to Christmas Day.

School was out for two weeks and we were spending quality time with our neighborhood friends. Our house was being decorated. Dad would bring home his usual Charlie Brown Christmas tree, which always infuriated my mother, but she would never say a word. Mom would be busy baking cookies days on end. Candles would burn throughout the house. Christmas songs by Jim Reeves and Dean Martin were playing nonstop.

Trimming the tree was a wonderful family tradition, with hot chocolate being served as we were beginning to place the long silver tinsel on the scattered branches. Stringing popcorn to decorate the tree was fun, but much of it never made it on the string. Mom and dad even placed a cardboard, red brick cutout fireplace against the east wall of our living room so Santa would have a way to bring the presents on Christmas morning.

Nevertheless, the best memory I have is the walnuts being brought out in the special Christmas bowl. The silver-colored nutcracker was placed along its side. I loved eating walnuts, but we only got them during Christmas season. I created my carefully devised hoarding strategy as I secretly took handfuls of the precious nuts and stashed them in my four-drawer, birch-colored dresser. I hid them behind my neatly folded shirts, which would ensure an availability of tasty treats for many weeks later.

Ultimately, my plan would fail. I was busted when my mom put my clean clothes away. My parents were never mad at me; instead, they were happy to solve the mystery of the missing walnuts. I actually think they were privately chuckling for weeks after as they enjoyed their morning coffee.

I still have my childhood dresser, now an antique, where I stowed away those dozens of walnuts. Those are fond memories of the past and, on occasion, they still put a little smirky grin on my face.

Chapter 3
TOBOGGAN RUN

It never took very much snow in the early winter months for me to pull out the toboggan from the old black tar-paper shed. The outbuilding was used to stockpile the broken lawnmowers and the many used and almost worn-out bicycles, and to store dozens of half-filled rusty paint cans. Mostly everything inside was junk, as nothing was ever thrown away.

The toboggan was old and noticeably well-used. The long, narrow boards were slightly cracked on both sides. It was six feet in

21

length, made of two-tone colored wooden oak. The curved front was slightly warped, but that was no big deal as you never could steer or turn the toboggan anyway.

Our sledding hill was in front of our house, where four large 50-foot Lombardy poplar trees stood towering and landmarking our two and a half acres of property. At the bottom of the hill, we needed to carefully maneuver our sled past the 12 randomly planted apple trees.

Speed was very important to us, so we meticulously packed down the snow on the hillside as hard as possible with vintage metal coal shovels. On occasion, we were able to sneak out buckets of water to further harden the surface.

The enjoyment of sledding was to discover new and more challenging hills. The older boys in our neighborhood clan, who were quite daring and of high energy, organized our one-mile trek to Rock Hill. The hill was an old ski slope on the University of Minnesota Duluth property, to which six of us towed two toboggans.

It was a night of sledding adventure with the full moon reflecting off the sparkling pure white snow. It seemed so bright, almost like it was mid-day. As we looked down from the summit of the hill we were awestruck and speechless. We had a high level of hesitation and a fair amount of indecision with our next move. Our final conclusion was made; we walked this far and no way we were going to chicken out now. The hill was much more vertical than we envisioned. There were many mature spruce trees lining both sides of the narrow pathway. We decided to go in tandem, one right after the other, three boys on each toboggan – counting "3, 2, 1 - go!"

The speed was faster than we could have ever imagined, and halfway down the hill we were veering off course, heading directly toward the first wave of towering trees. We all dove off just before impact, tumbling together and bouncing off the trunks of the trees. The toboggans came to rest by lodging between the many rows of timbers.

We all came out of it slightly bruised and shaken. Our faces were planted deeply in the bitterly cold snow. Rock Hill claimed victory over our challenge, and during our

walk back home we swore to each other to
never return.

Chapter 4
THE HIDDEN VALLEY

There were those special times when my friends and I would take a summer day and explore far beyond our neighborhood boundaries. We packed sandwiches and filled a Boy Scout-style canteen with water and took off on foot to discover the outside world.

The farthest we ever went as 9- or 10-year-olds, was the creek just behind the Little League field. Not far away was the castle on top of the hill. We didn't know it, but it was actually a private Benedictine college founded in 1912. There were two towers, north and south, protruding high in the sky -- a little like the witch's castle in the "Wizard of Oz."

The towers were designed in a Romanesque style with an exterior of igneous basalt stone, quarried from the Lake Superior basins. The stone is dark, dense and very strong.

We followed the overgrown trail on the west side of the creek, which led to the back of the college, where there were many headstones arranged in organized rows. The graveyard was well-groomed and the individual plots honored many past Benedictine Sisters of the St. Scholastica Monastery.

The trail was well-maintained and looped around to the south, where it met the edge of the hidden valley. The trail ended and we were in awe of the many slopes. We felt like the French explorer Daniel Greysolon, Sieur du Lhut in the 17th century as we walked blindly through this uncharted land.

There were many wonderful sounds of nature, with red squirrels chattering loudly as we approached their territory. Birds were plentiful, flying high above the tops of the trees.

We eventually maneuvered our way east and discovered the cliffs off of Kenwood Avenue. My friends carefully navigated down the steep rock ledges to the bottom. I, on the other hand, chose a safer route and walked around to the canopy of Norway spruces to the lower base.

We walked the roadway and the back streets home, sharing and talking about our many discoveries. It was a wonderful journey and a new adventure not to be forgotten by us young boys.

Chapter 5
RUNNING A BUSINESS

I was 10 years old when I took my first solo trip on the city bus to downtown Duluth. Every two weeks I was required to go to the Northwestern Bank of Commerce and pay the money I collected from my paper route customers. I would carefully organize my currency in the proper denominations in my dark blue zipper bag, which was given to me by the Duluth Herald daily paper.

I would catch the bus at Kenwood Shopping Center, hiding my money pouch in my oversized jacket. I was frightful during each trip that someone would notice it and attempt to take it from me.

Downtown Duluth, in my young eyes, was the most exciting place to go. It was a mecca for shopping, with many tall buildings side-by-side. Restaurants were plentiful and many stores had their own soda fountains. There were one-screen theaters with beautiful art deco designs, with large balconies overlooking the main floor. Bookstores and malt shops were abundant, with the F. W. Woolworth five and dime on the main corner in the center of town.

It was very difficult to find an available paper route as there were many young boys waiting in line, wanting to earn extra money. The routes always seemed to be passed down from friend to friend or brother to brother.

Rick, at 13 years old, was the carrier on West Arrowhead Road in the Kenwood neighborhood, which just happened to go right past my house. It was the route that I had spent a year asking for. Finally, in 1963, as the school year ended, I was offered the job. I found out quickly that I was required by Rick to work for free for over a month to learn all aspects of my new business. Finally, I was officially awarded Route 335E and became the carrier on West Arrowhead Road.

I was soon able to save enough money to purchase a 10-speed bicycle, which I had my eyes on for quite some time.

I delivered papers Monday through Friday at 4 p.m. each day. It didn't matter if it was cold out or pouring rain. During one of our typical June thunderstorms, papers still had to be delivered on time and in good condition.

It was a real business, and I saved a good amount of money. In the four years I ran my paper route, I collected almost every silver mercury dime you could find in Duluth. I bought old and rare coins from Stan, who owned a small rundown gold and silver shop on the eastern edge of downtown. I purchased a used, but very fast, go-kart and a 30-30 Marlin lever action deer rifle. Although my first purchase was a fortified metal lock box to keep my money and other valuables safe.

I sold those silver dimes in 1980 for $2 each, which paid for one year of tuition at the University of Minnesota Duluth.

Chapter 6
THE SECRET SPRING

On the northwest edge of our property line, nearby our apple orchard was a clearing where the sun shined and radiated its warmth during early summer days. I don't remember when I first discovered the wild strawberry patch, but it quickly became my secret place.

I would lay down in the soft grass for hours indulging in the sweet fruits of nature's bounty. My fingers were deeply stained red for many days afterwards. I recall our family rarely had fresh fruit from the grocery store.

When we were hungry, we foraged outside and enjoyed the abundance of plums, apples, rhubarb, raspberries and chokecherries.

The five-acre property next to us had been an old gravel pit years ago, now overgrown with wild bushes and aspen trees. I often found myself exploring the land and wondering about its history. On the west edge of the pit, bordering the Paavolas' woods, was a large, reddish-colored boulder, maybe four feet tall, more oval in shape than round. It may have been my youthful imagination, but I clearly remember there was an old Native American carving of a woodpecker on one of its sides. Throughout my childhood it became a meeting place with friends and was forever known as Woodpecker Rock.

In the lower portion of the Paavolas' woods was a swamp with northern white cedar trees on the outer edge. A coniferous forest wetland covered 1,000 square feet of the woods. Black spruce and balsam fir surrounded the many patches of marsh ferns. Sedge grass was prominent along the muddy, well-used game trail that led us to a drinking spring.

The spring was a natural phenomenon, bubbling crystal-clear water up from the earth. It didn't seem like it should be there, but it was. We often drank from it with no hesitation; it was our fountain of youth. An old metal ladle was eventually tied onto a cedar branch nearby. We had only heard rumors that it was safe to drink, but it didn't matter to us. It was our special place to help quench our thirst from the summer heat.

Chapter 7
CLIFF ROCK

To the north of the woods at the edge of the Paavolas' five acres of land was an old and narrow creek bed that remained dry for most of the year. Nearby was a ridgeline that went to the west for miles beyond. It was covered with beautiful yellow birch trees, which stood up to 60 feet tall. The yellowish-brown bark was shiny, with large portions of horizontal raised pores.

The trees were scattered and the sun shone through them, with its luminous rays gently reflecting off the forest floor. The trees gave the impression that they each possessed their own personality as they stood solitary on the gentle slope.

Following the ridgeline, there was an old foundation which was overcome by brush and small saplings.   There was nothing left except a few broken cement blocks and rusted metal pieces scattered about in the hole in the ground. There were no roads or noticeable trails to the ramshackle, abandoned structure. It was in the middle of the woods and its past will certainly never be known. Further to the west, maybe half a mile or so, was a sizeable rock formation mostly covered with dark green cap moss. The rocks were large, one on top of another and their numerous crevasses were deep into the stone. The fissures were wide and certainly an ideal place for numerous small game to call home.

The rock formation dropped steeply to a vast clearing of wild flowers. To reach the bottom where the daisies were plentiful, you needed to carefully maneuver the steep bank by holding onto the protruding branches of the nearby trees.

The discovery of Cliff Rock came from one of many adventures exploring the woods with my neighborhood friends. It became our place where we would often go to hang out for many hours at a time. We often contemplated how it stood so still and tall in the middle of nowhere and how it found its place.

Chapter 8
FAIRMONT PARK

The 40-acre Fairmont parkland was purchased by the City of Duluth in 1901 for $4,000. The park is located in the heart of western Duluth, at 72nd Avenue West and Grand Avenue.

Kingsbury Creek, with its steep banks and large crevasse basalt boulders, flows rapidly through the middle of the park. The creek is named after William Wallace Kingsbury, a Pennsylvania native who built a modest cabin on the Fairmont land sometime after

1852. Kingsbury later became a member of the U.S. House of Representatives from the Minnesota Territory. He died at the age of 63 in Tarpon Springs, Florida.

Over the years, foot bridges, picnic tables and benches were added to the park. Trails were interwoven throughout the white pine forest and a beautiful standalone pavilion was built on the flattest portion of the property.

The numerous deeper pools of the creek provided the perfect spot for many children to cool off from the summer heat.

The park soon became highly popular for family gatherings and labor union outings.

In 1923, a single pen was built for Bert Onsgard's pet deer. Bert's vision for the Lake Superior Zoo had begun. Soon after, Pittsburgh Steel Company donated fencing, and nearby citizens contributed a variety of exotic animals. A successful fundraising campaign allowed for the purchase of a pair of lion cubs. Soon, the zoo consumed 16 acres of picturesque scenery of Fairmont Park.

Underneath the rolls of tall pines were multiple stainless steel horse troughs full of ice-cold pop. This was a simple dream come true as I was frantically searching through the mountain of ice for a bottle of Hires Root Beer.

This excursion was certainly one of many highlights of the dog days of summer. It was our annual trip to the Painters' Picnic at Fairmont Park. My dad had been a union painter since his early 20s, which provided a modest living for our family.

Volunteers were diligently cooking neat columns of hot dogs and hamburgers on a large homemade iron grill. There were tins full of corn on the cob and an endless amount of potato chips.

There were different events for children throughout the day. I participated in many of them and I even won a blue ribbon in a running race.

These were the simple and joyous days of one young boy's life.

Chapter 9
RUSTY THE TOM CAT

I was always exploring the fields, the
swamps or nearby woods. I enjoyed
watching the birds during their spring and
fall migrations or observing the ducks
nesting in the back swamps. I could spend
hours looking up in the sky, being
captivated by the shapes and movements of
the clouds. Occasionally, I would witness a
majestic bald eagle gliding effortlessly in
circles looking for its next prey while I was
catching tadpoles and frogs. The hawks of

all different sorts were plentiful, as were many other bird species.

When I was tired, I would lay down in the backyard looking for the elusive four-leaf clover and, shortly afterwards, fall asleep in the uncut grass. Upon waking up, I would climb the highest tree in the neighborhood and then feast on raspberries on the west slope near our apple orchard.

These were precious moments that I spent alone.

One summer afternoon I found an evening grosbeak with a broken wing. I quickly brought it home and it became a valuable member of our family for a decade.

On one special autumn evening, I heard a cat screeching on the outskirts of our backyard. I went to take a closer look and discovered a larger-than-life orange colored tomcat. It was hurt and definitely in pain. I knew I needed to rescue him and he allowed me to carry him back home.

The cat laid still in the box for days with old bath towels providing a bed for his comfort. My mother, Mary, had a soft touch and a very kind heart for animals. I knew he would also become a member of our family. I named him Rusty after his bright orange hues.

Years later, Rusty went on one of his adventures, but this time he never returned. I cried for days.

Chapter 10
THE ELUSIVE HAZELNUTS

The beaked hazelnut shrubs grow wild in the western Great Lakes region and are often found under the birch and aspen canopies in northern Minnesota. The green husks are covered with prickly bristles and begin to ripen as the summer season changes to the cooler autumn months. When the husks start to brown, the squirrels, chipmunks and mice take aim to harvest one of their favorite treats.

During one late-September day, while I was exploring deep in the woods, east of our back property, I found the remnants of an old Boy Scout camp. There were time-worn boards and corroded sheet metal mostly covered with overgrown brush. Tin cookware and rusty cans were scattered about. I had found my secret treasure chest, full of many past memories hidden in the woods. I was positive no one had come across my revelation for many decades.

In my course of discovery, I came across a hazelnut bush only a few yards from the cluttered camp. I was curious what they were and I picked a few to show my parents.

I was told they were hazelnuts and that they were ripe for picking. Days later, I returned and cleaned the shrubs bare of my newly discovered nut. After dehulling them, they were placed on a baking sheet and put in the oven for 10 minutes. Picking the hazelnuts became a yearly tradition for me and a tasty snack for my family.

Chapter 11
SATURDAY NIGHT BATH

Saturday nights were special for me and my friends, as it was sauna night. First, we would gather in the Paavolas' basement and play a few games of pool. The table was well-used and the green velvet was so thin and worn out you could almost see the top layer of plywood. None of us had any complaint, though, as this was the only pool table in the neighborhood. We were grateful for a place to hang out without any intrusions.

Gerty and Ray Paavola, my friend Marty's parents, were glad to host the neighborhood boys. They both knew we would all be safe there and I think that brought them a sense of comfort.

There was never an argument among us boys. We just had fun and enjoyed our younger days to the fullest!

We were waiting for our turn to take our Saturday night bath in the well-constructed, traditional, wood-burning Finnish sauna. Ray would carefully stoke the stove with dried hardwood from his backwoods.

Ray and Gerty would always go first and when their spirits and souls were refreshed it would be our turn.

I learned from the Paavolas at a very young age that every Saturday night throughout Finland was sauna night. It was a ritual for cleaning your body, but more importantly for relaxing and socializing. Stories were always told, some true and some exaggerated or at least sensationalized.

We were butt-naked and always sat on the top bench for maximum heat. Marty would

often take the wooden ladle out of the water
bucket and saturate the hot coals.

There were always fresh-cut aromatic cedar
boughs for us to softly beat over our body
In the winter months, we would always jump
and roll in the fresh fallen snow for a cooling
effect. Our saunas would last for over an
hour, and when we became of legal drinking
age there were plenty of Budweisers being
iced down in an old five-gallon bucket.

The night would end with us playing cards in
the basement and drinking banana
milkshakes.

These traditions are now lost with time, but
the memories will never be forgotten.

Chapter 12
NIGHT SKIING

The wooden skis were well-worn and seven feet long, with a narrowing, pointed tip at the front. They were made of durable hickory wood, and the old bindings were unembellished with frayed leather straps. The poles were made of inexpensive bamboo.

On a cold night in 1965, we trekked our favorite trail, which crossed the frozen Chester Creek near the back 40 acres of the private Catholic college on the hill. The path weaved narrowly through the birch and

49

aspen for nearly a quarter-mile. We packed the snow down with our skis as we worked our way up to the trailhead.

The full moon was immense and bright, and the sky was showcasing its countless stars. The forest was glistening off the fresh fallen snow.

This would be one of our many skiing trips in the woods. It didn't matter to us how steep and winding the trail was or if we were insane to even attempt to ski down the hill without thinking of our odds of crashing into the trees. It was an adventure that we all embraced, to try and accomplish the impossible.

That night, after a dozen noble attempts, none of us fulfilled our dream of making it to the bottom. We laughed and we cried during this memorable night in the woods.

Our friendship and loyalty to each other were once again confirmed as we headed back home with our skis firmly settled on our shoulders. Night skiing with best friends will be a memory I will never forget as long as I live.

Rest in peace, Paavola boys …

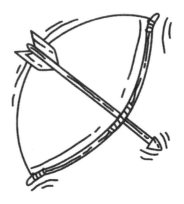

Chapter 13
ARROWS IN THE SKY

During Christmas Eve in 1963, my eyes quickly burst with joy, out of their sockets, as I was opening my present. It was a bow and arrow set which I could only have dreamed of receiving. I would now begin to plan my upcoming hunting trips in the nearby woods. The grouse were plentiful, and I had often seen or heard them drumming under the many towering cedar trees in the Paavolas' woods.

Rabbits were abundant in our back property, and I knew the special trick to stop them in their tracks. I would whistle at a very high pitch, and they would immediately be frozen in place. I would then have a clear and easy shot at my prey. My dad would be thrilled and proud of me for bringing home any type of wild game for supper.

I had previously made bows and arrows from aspen saplings. After cutting the young trees down with my hatchet, I would carefully peel back a thin layer of bark to uncover the white undercoating. You could smell and I often tasted the sweet inner sap, which would be slowly running down to the bottom of the trunk.

The bow would be crudely formed with notches on both ends, where the string was tied tightly. Arrows were made from the straightest branches and carved until they were suitable for flight. A sharp point was whittled carefully on the tip of one end.

The homemade bows were fun to make but the arrows flew wildly and rarely hit their desired target. I would walk through the deep woods pretending to be a great hunter of past years.

After the extended winter subsided and the summer days became long, I had become very accurate with my Christmas bow. One beautiful June day, my friends and I took my weapon to the woods. We began to shoot at stumps of fallen trees, and I even launched an arrow at a racketing red squirrel and missed. Somehow, we came up with not such a great idea -- to shoot an arrow at the sky. We watched the arrow reach its peak and, as it started to descend to Earth, we panicked and ran in different directions. When no one was hurt, we each took a turn and, after a few close calls, the game of arrows in the sky wisely ended.

Throughout my childhood, the neighboring woods was my playground. There were no worries, only unforgettable and good memories of my youth.

Chapter 14
WINTER STORMS

The meteorological winter months in northern Minnesota are December, January and February. Although Mother Nature often ignored those 90 days on the calendar in my childhood years.

For some reason, Mother Nature would plot with Old Man Winter and include March and November in our long, cold and snowy winters. During my youth, the total annual accumulation of snow was over seven feet, or maybe it was eight feet.

If you grew up in the 1950s and 60s in the North Star State, you certainly can remember how those heavenly and cosmic white snow crystals would never stop. The northeast winds off the greatest of the Great Lakes would compact the fresh fallen snow into hardened snowdrifts up to 10 feet tall.

When I was in junior high school, I had to walk two miles to and from school. Rain, sleet or snow -- those were the days.

The roof on my house was constructed just right to gather even more of those huge and well-packed drifts of snow. By mid-winter, I would lean an old broken wooden ladder against the house and climb up to begin the task of removing tons of snow before it collapsed into our living room. After hours of carefully shoveling without digging into the fragile asphalt shingles, I took a leap of faith and jumped off the roof into the deep snow.

I am almost positive my dad never shoveled an ounce of snow, once his children were able to grasp a shovel's wooden handle. I distinctly remember in one of his rant and raves being told the reason he had children was for them to do the many outdoor chores.

During these big winter storms, I developed a love-hate relationship with them. Early in the morning my mother would be listening to Pat Cadigan on KDAL radio to find out if there were any school closings. She would be cooking salt pork and eggs for dad while they were both drinking Folgers coffee and smoking Winston cigarettes.

I was elated when I received the news that school was closed for the day. For sure we would be outside sledding with our neighborhood friends. My jubilation would be short-lived as dad took charge of our free time once the storm eased. The old, metal shovels were placed evenly on the front porch. Our priority would now be to clear 600 feet of snow on our long class-five gravel driveway so dad could go to work the following day.

There were many hours of shoveling with my heavy winter coat and boots on to keep warm. My reward afterwards would be a hot cup of cocoa. The snow days back then weren't so much fun, but maybe I developed a little work ethic and character.

Today, I only have a 100-foot driveway, and for some reason I love shoveling and making it the cleanest driveway in the neighborhood.

Chapter 15
THE MILKY WAY

I grew up in a very small house, which was set back far from the main roadway. At night, well past sunset, it was pitch black outside, with almost no light pollution nearby. Fireflies were abundant in our yard and I would often take a Mason jar to catch a few of them as they flew erratically about. They would always be released back to nature shortly afterwards.

As I would look up towards the sky, I could clearly see the beautiful spiral Milky Way galaxy. It was so vast, with over a billion stars glowing far away. Earth and our sun are located in the Orion Arm, about two-thirds from its center of our galaxy. I have vivid memories of seeing the distinctive array of yellows and blues. The brightness in the heavens was so spectacular for me to witness and wonder of its origin. What intrigued me the most was the cosmos; our universe never ends. I just wanted to understand why, at my young age.

In my early teens, I purchased a modest telescope with some of my savings. I wanted to learn and identify the stars in the constellations. I enjoyed looking at the deep craters of the moon that were formed by the bounteous asteroids and comets. In a very small way, I felt I was the famous 17th century Italian astronomer Galileo, discovering planets and their moons in our galaxy.

I was thrilled when I was first able to find the star Polaris. I would locate the two stars at the end of the Big Dipper's cup, then I pointed down to the tip of the Little Dipper's handle. The North Star was noticeably brighter than the other stars in the Ursa Minor constellation. It marks the point in the night sky in which anyone could easily identify the direction of due north.

On special occasions, when timing was perfect, I would witness a rare satellite flying harmlessly across our celestial sphere. My eyes would fixate on it until it disappeared into darkness. I enjoyed reading science fiction books and contemplated where other life would be in our endless universe.

Today, day or night, I am often looking at the sky, hoping to witness a shooting star or see a majestic bald eagle in flight.

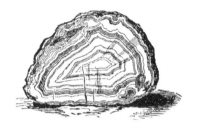

Chapter 16
AGATE HUNTING

10,000 years ago, glaciers carried agates far from their origins in the Lake Superior region throughout the state of Minnesota. Agates are frequently found on the shores of Lake Superior, river banks and in the many rural gravel pits.

Lake Superior agates are stained by iron ore and are a gemstone consisting of chalcedony and quartz, and were formed within volcanic and metamorphic rocks over one billion years ago. They are translucent and rich in many colors, including black, red, white, green, blue, yellow, purple and orange.

The highly treasured eye agate has perfectly round bands, or "eyes," dotting the surface of the rare stone. Agates are extremely hard rocks that have the ability to retain a highly polished surface.

My mother would pack bologna sandwiches and potato chips into a picnic basket, along with a thermos of coffee and a jug of Kool-Aid as refreshments for our many adventures to the gravel pits on the northwest side of Rice Lake Road. There are numerous fishing lakes nearby, where our family would spend many Saturday mornings attempting to catch the Minnesota state fish, the walleye.

My two brothers and I would pile in the back bed of dad's work truck. My mother and sister Patti would join dad up front in the single cab. Back in the 1950s and 60s there wasn't even a second thought about the safety of riding in the back of a truck. It was the only way to transport the family or half of the Little League team.

The gravel pit was not gated and was open for anyone who was willing to search for the perfect stone. I am sure dad only agreed to look for the precious agates because mom loved it so much. My mother always seemed to find the biggest and most colorful agates. I will always remember her yell of joy when she found a treasure. She would spit on her find and quickly rub the dirt off so the colors would appear and shine. I am not sure I spent much time looking for agates during our trips to the gravel pits. I do remember climbing up the mountains of rock and sliding down on my backend. Getting dirty was normal for me and I loved running around every inch of the pit's acres. Lunch was served near the row of boulders where mom would showcase her prize finds.

My mother's brother, Uncle Hank, was an agate collector and polished his cherished rocks in a small electric tumbler designed to bring out nature's colors to the fullest. It would take at least a month of tumbling before they were finished. My mother eventually purchased her own tumbler and polishing rocks became a very important hobby for her.

Agate hunting, fishing and being with her dogs were mother's true "joys" in her life. She joined the workforce at 44 years old as the head cook at a local hospital. She loved every minute of it; she especially loved teaching the college girls how to cook and prepare dinners for the many hospital patients.

Mary Keenan was a petite 5 foot, 3 inches tall. She died of lung disease at the early age of 66. I visit and clean my parents' cemetery site each spring. They are resting in peace, side by side in a military plot in front of the flagpole.

Chapter 17
THE NEXT-DOOR NEIGHBOR

The Wasbotten family lived next door to us on West Arrowhead Road. Ricky was two years older than me and Bruce was one year younger. Their father, Dick, had a sizable woodworking shop just behind the narrow two-story home. I remember when I was 8 or 9 years old, I would help clean up the mounds of sawdust and scrap wood for a chocolate malt at Boyce Drug Store's ice cream fountain. No money was ever exchanged -- just a few hours of hard work for a special treat.

The Keenans, Wasbottens, Paavolas and Swapinskis all lived within two blocks of each other. We were childhood friends and our friendships continued throughout our adult lives.

The Wasbottens' home was built on a steep hill with a lengthy driveway to the bottom. One winter afternoon, Bruce and I came up with a new sledding plan. We pulled my toboggan to the top of the driveway, a foot away from the busy roadway. The driveway was lightly snow-covered and icy, which provided a perfect runway for a fast toboggan ride.

One-third of the way down the hill, Grandpa "Ole" Wasbotten walked out of the side door of his house directly in our path.

Unfortunately, we were unable to stop or turn the toboggan in time. We knocked him over and he went flying through the air for many yards down the steep slope. Both of us were in shock and we couldn't believe what just happened.

Grandpa Wasbotten survived the crash and we immediately endured his many harsh Norwegian words. Bruce and I were extremely scared and we quickly realized how much trouble we were in. Never again did we attempt a toboggan ride down the steep and icy Wasbotten driveway.

In the Wasbottens' back property was an old industrial blasting mat operation. They would pick up thousands of old worn tires from service stations across the Northland. Tires were stacked in mountain-high piles throughout the property. Workers would slice the tires in quarter sections with a large shear machine that could easily cut your hand off with the slightest mistake. The quarter pieces would then have holes punched on opposite sides to be strung through two thick cables. When the large mats were completed, they would be hoisted up by a huge wooden crane and stacked outside. The blasting mats were eventually sold around the country where dynamite was used for construction projects.

The rubber holes that were punched through the tires were collected by neighborhood kids to be used as ammunition for our homemade slingshots.

Life was simple growing up in our neighborhood, but we never seemed to have a dull moment.

Chapter 18
UNCLE UNO

In the late 1950s and 1960s, Uncle Uno and Aunt Marcella would always set aside Friday evenings for grocery shopping at the Kenwood Red Owl. Marcella was one of my dad's older sisters. After my uncle and aunt finished their weekly shopping, they would come to our house for a visit. Uno would always bring a Sara Lee cream pie to share with our family.

My mother would be preparing Chef Boyardee box pizzas. The contents included a small can of tomato sauce, yeast, flour,

Parmesan cheese and a packet of parsley. Mother would add slices of pepperoni and a few other ingredients from the refrigerator.

It was Pizza and TV Night!

We would all settle down in our small living room, which featured one wall covered from floor to ceiling with well-aged, nicotine-stained, wood paneling. Silhouette pictures of each child were hanging proudly from the wall. The adults would sit on the rectangle floral-pattern chairs and couch with TV trays in front of them. Children were sprawled across the floor.

The television was on, with an old rabbit ear antenna delicately adjusted for the best picture possible. Uncle Uno's favorite Friday night programs were the Smothers Brothers and The Jackie Gleason Show.

Uncle Uno was a sergeant in the U.S. Army during World War II in the European Theatre. He had many talents that truly amazed me as a young child, none more than his masterful accordion playing. He would often bring over his odd-looking box-like instrument with keys and buttons on either side. He would move the two sides back and forth to create a strange but beautiful sound.

In the summer months, Uno would always bring over his flimsy, thin layered first baseman's glove to play catch. The neighborhood boys would join me in the backyard as Uno would toss the baseball high in the sky for us to scramble after. It was a point game we played. Players would receive 75 points for catching a popup, 50 points for a line drive and 25 points for a grounder. The first boy to 500 points would be declared the winner.

I have no memories of my grandparents, so in many ways Marcella and Uno were my grandparents. Both of them were a very important part of my life as I was growing up. They would always attend family birthdays, special occasions and holidays.

Uno was a Mr. Fixit guy who could repair almost anything. I have a distant memory of Uno fixing vintage motor boat engines in his garage. He loved to sing and he is remembered by many for his boisterous laugh.

Marcella was a woman who never had an enemy. She died at a young age in 1972 from complications of diabetes. Uno truly enjoyed life to the fullest and died at the age of 87 in 2006. I went to his funeral and cried.

Chapter 19
CATHOLIC CHURCH

The shortcut trail was small, but well-defined and crossed an open field adjacent to our property line. On occasion, as I passed by, a startled pheasant would take flight from the nearby shrubbery. The trail continued through the woods behind a narrow two-story home, which had seen better days many years ago. The trail became a path that crossed a small meadow, where sunrays shone brightly and wild raspberries were plentiful on both sides. Just ahead, there was a geological rock cropping of exposed bedrock overlooking the grassy area of the Catholic church parking lot.

The location for our weekly tackle football games was perfect for us, as the clearing was wide with well-maintained grass. The parking lot lights allowed us to play after sunset and it was about 50 yards long.

Boys from all different neighborhoods would show up at a pre-determined time. Teams would be divided mostly by friendships and age. Numerous footballs would be brought; no one would wear helmets or pads. The games would last for hours or until there was an injury or minor skirmish.

The priest from the church lived no more than 200 feet from our playing field. We were never asked to stop our games or to leave the property. It seemed we were well-accepted as the boys of the neighborhood having harmless fun.

The grassy area of the church parking lot became one of our playgrounds throughout my childhood. It was the center of our different neighborhoods for us to meet and enjoy the fall season of football.

When the games ended, we all went our separate ways. I took my half-mile shortcut back home, just in time for supper.

Chapter 20
READY OR NOT,
HERE I COME

Hide-and-seek has roots dating many centuries ago and has been traced back as far as the ancient Greeks. I have a vivid memory of being a young child growing up in Duluth and playing hide-and-seek on Friday evenings. Neighborhood friends and my first cousins would gather at our home when the sun set, with the moon and stars shining brightly. We lived far back from the main roadway, where there was an eerie feeling, but it was a perfect backdrop for children's nighttime games.

We often played many other old school games such as "Annie, Annie, over," kick the can and tag. We played these simple games because our options were limited but surely were wonderful moments in my life.

Mother would always end the evening by handing out her homemade Kool-Aid pops.

As we played hide-and-seek there would be one player chosen to close their eyes against one of the large Lombardy poplar trees. The seeker counted to 50 and everyone else swiftly scattered throughout the yard hiding behind any structure that could be found. "48, 49, 50!" the seeker would yell out as loud as possible. "Ready or not, here I come!" The seeker would quickly scan the grounds attempting to find the cloaked players. The last player found would be declared the winner and the first person found would be the next seeker.

There are other versions of how to play the game, but it didn't matter to us. We were all running around getting exercise.

A perfect way to end our day before
bedtime.

Chapter 21
GO-KART RACING

I don't exactly remember when I first began my infatuation with racing and feeling the exhilaration of high speeds. I was young though, maybe 9 or 10 years of age.

In the Duluth area there were two separate go-kart tracks. The first one was located on the city's northern outskirts, on Calvary Road. The second location was in the rural west and secluded area of Duluth, which is now made up of malls and brick and mortar shopping outlets.

The price for the three-minute ride was 50 cents. I always had a contemplative approach before I purchased my ticket. I would carefully observe the speed of the multi-colored go-karts to pinpoint the fastest one. With my ticket in hand, I would rush to be the first in line to ensure my choice of kart. My driving competence could be best described as cautiously aggressive. I had little or no fear of going fast and darting between two other karts as we approached the straightaway. There were never any collisions in my many rides -- only close calls!

I would often fantasize that I was racing a stock car at the county fairgrounds in Proctor.

The following summer, with my paper route savings, I purchased my own go-kart. The frame was primitively made with old iron tubing, which was welded hastily at the seams. The motor was a two-stroke combustion Homelite engine, which was firmly bolted on the rear mounting plate.

My go-kart was low to the ground and could easily hit 40 miles per hour. It was fast. I had my parental permission to ride around our house, but it was short-lived after I tore up the lawn.

In the weeks after my purchase, I was able to construct a crude track on the gentle slopes in the front field of our house. This was a memorable period of my early years.

It was a good life with many simple joys.

Chapter 22
MOTHER GOES FISHING

Thousands of years ago, the slow-moving and powerful continental glacier rearranged the landscape of Minnesota's territory. The topography was altered significantly, allowing the glacier melt and rainfall to be captured in the forming of more than 10,000 lakes.

One of the many joys of living in Minnesota is fishing in one of those plentiful lakes. Anglers' prize catch would be the walleye, Minnesota's state fish. Walleyes are abundant and thrive in the northern states and Canada. The fish is a delicacy to many and when cooked, it has a tasty pure white flaky flesh.

Fish Lake Reservoir is a part of the Cloquet and St. Louis River aquatic ecosystem. The lake and its flowage is approximately 3,000 square acres and has 45 miles of shoreline. Fish Lake is located 20 miles northwest from the heart of Duluth, Minnesota.

This was often our family's lake of choice for our fishing outings. Virginia Keenan, my dad's older sister, would often rent, for a week, a well-used but clean cabin on the lake at Eagle's Nest Resort. This would be our perfect summer vacation. We would fish and swim until twilight. The weather always seemed to be perfect. Food was plentiful throughout the day, with bottled pop of all flavors being iced in an old metal wash bucket.

Mother was a very petite woman with wavy blonde hair and pure blue eyes. She would wear a light cotton rounded style hat while searching for the perfect shoreline spot to cast her lure. She would use her own Zebco fishing reel with a six-foot fishing pole. Her accuracy with each throw was as perfect as any professional's. You could see the joy on her face as she relished her private time on the rocky shore.

Mother was always very patient when she was fishing. I would often watch her from a distance when she would hook into a fish, which was often a keeper walleye. Mother's excitement was like a child's emotion when catching their first fish. Her exhilaration would soon be shared by everyone in the camp.

Her smile was a delight to witness. Mother passed away at the young age of 66.

Love you, mom!

Chapter 23
THE GREEN BUMBOAT

I was 15 years old when I was hitchhiking from my Kenwood neighborhood to the YMCA in downtown Duluth. On a Saturday afternoon I could always find a pick-up basketball game at the Y with other boys my own age.

During this era, it was quite common to stick out your thumb and catch a free ride to your desired destination. There were no worries or even second thoughts of danger.

On that summer afternoon, it only took a few minutes before a large, newer style blue Buick pulled over and asked me where I was going. After a brief exchange of words, I got my lift.

The gentleman was old and meek looking. He had grayish hair and was smoking a small cigarette that looked like a cigar. His name was Lawrence Kaner and he explained that he was the owner and operator of a 55-foot supply boat that tied up to the many ore carriers that would berth at the docks on the industrial western edge of Duluth.

The ore boats were plentiful and over 700 feet long. They would be loaded with many tons of taconite pellets, a byproduct of the magnetite ore. Almost mile-long trains would rumble loudly on the aging tracks from the deep pit mines on northern Minnesota's Iron Range.

The Port of Duluth-Superior is North America's farthest inland freshwater seaport. It is protected by over nine miles of natural breakwater shelters, which host over 20 privately owned bulk cargo docks.

During the drive downtown, Kaner offered me a job; my pay would be $5 per hour. I accepted immediately and suddenly I became the first mate on the green bumboat at my young age.

My job responsibilities included securing the ropes to the ore boat's decking with large protruding gaft hooks. I would then set up a well-worn wooden ladder for the sailors to climb down to replenish their needed supplies in the lower level.

The bumboat was a compacted department store, with many shelves loaded with all types and sizes of warm clothes and rain gear. Insulated boots were stacked high and scattered on the floors through the aisles. Magazines, books, candies and chips were plentiful. There was almost everything you could imagine on the bumboat.

I was also responsible for stocking the shelves, cleaning and occasionally running the cash register. Kaner was mostly operating his illegal dice game for all those who wanted to gamble with him.

I made a little extra cash by sneaking beer into the sailors' quarters and placing the cans in the tank portion of their toilets. Bags of chips were always placed on top of the beer, hopefully disguising the obviously rectangular shaped 12-pack.

I was caught one time when the captain of the boat approached me as I was walking the deck. He said, "Son, what is in the bag?" My response was, "Groceries, sir." He then ripped the paper bag open and the beer crashed on the hard metal surface. That was my last delivery for the day.

The most enjoyable aspect of my job was my galley privileges. When business was slow, I was allowed to visit the galley and feast on the most wonderful food I have ever tasted. One time the chief steward sliced a large portion of meat and placed it between two pieces of warm homemade bread. It was the most tender and juicy sandwich I ever had. I had never tasted anything like it. I asked what kind of meat it was. He shouted out that it was a slice of pork roast.

The only type of pork I had ever had before was my mother's overcooked, micro-thin chops. They were barely edible.

The galley was the heart of the boat. It provided the necessary joy to the sailors during their long voyages on the Great Lakes.

My first mate career ended when the school year began in the fall. I continued to work for Kaner by shoveling his driveway during the winter months for extra money.

Chapter 24
HE'S SAFE

I thoroughly rubbed mink oil into my baseball glove weekly and the pocket became soft and perfectly formed into the shape of a hardball. I loved the smell of the rich oil as it penetrated deeply into the worn leather. It was the smell of playing America's game – there was nothing better. I would take my glove to bed at night and dream about my next game.

Like many boys growing up in the 1960s, I played baseball and I often played it all day long. We fantasized that we were Mickey

91

Mantle, Hank Aaron, Willie Mays or Harmon Killebrew. They were our heroes and we could only hope that someday we would also be playing in the major leagues.

When I was young, the highlight of my summer and fall days would be to sit a few feet away from our smaller RCA black and white dial television to watch the Minnesota Twins play. I rarely missed a game.

I can clearly remember those amazing and comical Minnesota Twins Hamm's Beer commercials. They featured the Hamm's Bear with the catchy jingle. From the Land of Sky Blue Waters – the beer was made in St Paul, Minnesota, and was sold throughout the Upper Midwest. Baseball was paramount in my life and remains my favorite sport today. I will always be a Minnesota Twins fan.

When I was 9 years old, I started to play baseball in Little League. My dad, Chester Keenan, was the coach for a few of those early years. He truly loved coaching and when we won a game, he treated the whole team to a 10-cent Coke at Boyce Drug Store.

Dad never argued with the umpires, but I do remember those occasional games when he waved his hands in front of his eyes. His intent was to send a message to the umpire that he missed the call. There was never a verbal exchange.

When I was 11 years old, I moved up to the majors in Little League. The players were more advanced in their skill level. I played second base or anywhere in the outfield. When boys turned 13, they were required to try out for one of the Babe Ruth teams. I was chosen by a new start-up team from the Duluth Heights. This was a minor ordeal for me as I was hoping to be picked by my neighborhood Kenwood team.

In the summer of 1968, at the age of 15, our team was dismantled because of a lack of players. I was chosen by another Duluth Heights team, the Red Sox. During the last game of the regular season, I was patiently sitting on the shabby green pine bench hoping to have my name called. This was an important game as the winning team would advance to the state tournament in the Twin Cities.

It was the bottom of the ninth inning with two outs when Coach House called my name. I entered the game as a pinch-runner for my teammate on third base.

I wasn't the fastest runner on the bench, but I think coach was confident I would meticulously follow his detailed instructions. Everyone on both teams knew House had a plan for me to steal home. After a fake attempt, hoping the catcher would throw the ball wildly back to third base, the play would be on. As the pitcher was in his windup, I sprinted as fast as I could to home plate and stopped three feet in front of the catcher, who had the ball in his mitt. I turned back and started to run to third and counted "one, two, three" as the ball whistled by my left ear. I quickly turned again, darted the other way and slid safely into home to win the game.

Joyous memories of baseball.

Chapter 25
THE NEIGHBORHOOD

The elementary school was only a few
blocks from the center of the neighborhood.
The Catholic and Lutheran churches were
across the street from each other and about
300 feet from the school. The Kenwood
Shopping Center was a city block south of
the two churches. The anchor businesses
were a drug and hardware store, Red Owl
grocery store and a small barbershop.

Nearby was a candy store, which we always
called the pink store. My favorite treat was
the yard-long shoestring strawberry licorice,

sold for a penny.   When I had extra money, I purchased a pack or two of baseball cards with a piece of Bazooka gum inside.

Duffy's, a burger joint, was located next to the shopping center and was the hangout for the older kids. Many of us who were younger stayed away, but on hot summer days we were found sitting at the soda fountain in the back of the drug store. Cherry Cokes and chocolate phosphates were among my favorite drinks and were sold for only a dime.

The baseball field was a short bicycle ride from my house. Almost every boy who grew up in Kenwood played on the Little League team.

Chester Creek was found winding through the nearby woods, just beyond the center field fence. There was a free-flowing drinking spring that poured from a stainless-steel pipe at the creek's edge.

Texaco, Skelly and DX were the three service stations and located at the crossroads of Kenwood Avenue and Arrowhead Road. Gas cost 31.9 cents per gallon.

During the winter months, the skating rinks were flooded at the elementary school. The roughly constructed wooden warming shack's stove was burning dried hardwood to keep children of all ages toasty as they laced up their skates.

The air force base in Duluth closed its operations on April 1,1969. There was an enormous military housing complex with over 100 acres of land for the service members and their families to stay. It was known to everyone in the area as the Capehart Housing Complex. It was located a half-mile from Kenwood Avenue on West Arrowhead Road. There was a large baseball field near the top of the hill in the housing area. During my Little League and Babe Ruth years, I clearly remember during our games a military truck would slowly drive along the street spraying the pesticide DDT and leaving a thick fog mass behind. The games were temporarily postponed until the fog dissipated.

During one summer of my youth, I came across a money-making scheme. At the time, there were many contractors working on the buildings throughout Capehart. I filled up a large thermos of Kool-Aid and rode my bicycle there during lunchtime. My new business was an immediate success and all summer long I delivered cool drinks to the thirsty workers.

This was our small community; it was only a half-mile in radius. We played with friends, rode our bicycles all day long and made bows and arrows from small aspen saplings. We skied in the woods and explored everywhere possible. We made up games and camped overnight in the Paavolas' woods. We were always on the run and discovering many new joys in our young lives. I will always remember my neighborhood and drinking those special Cherry Cokes at the local drug store.

IN CLOSING

I often reflect on my early years of life, when I spent so many special moments with my neighborhood friends. We were the Kenwood boys!

We discovered at a very early age the transcendental spirit of the nearby woods. We saw and felt the beauty nature provided us each day. We played all kinds of sports in the fields and parks. We were lucky to be able to enjoy the outdoors all day during those precious summer months. We made up games to have fun. We built homemade bows and arrows and sling shots. We all carried jackknives in our pockets. We built forts and treehouses and were lucky to be able to take a Finnish sauna on Saturday nights.

It was a wonderful era to grow up in. We were considered a poor family, but none of us knew it. We worked for our own money, as there was no such thing as a weekly allowance.

It was a wonderful life and I still miss going to the Boyce Drug Store and sitting at the soda fountain while enjoying one of their Cherry Cokes.

Thank you for reading my book. Hopefully, this will help you remember the special moments from your youth.

Good night, and find peace in your life.
Scott Keenan

ABOUT THE AUTHOR

My life as a child was a joyfully simple one, and the journey continued after those early years. Following high school, I joined the Minnesota Air National Guard during the Vietnam War. I ran my first mile at Lackland Air Force Base in San Antonio, Texas, in calf-high combat boots on a three-inch red sand track.

After 13 weeks of training, I retired home to Duluth and soon became a long-distance runner. In 1973, I was voted the next president of the North Shore Striders Running Club. Four years later, in 1977, I was the founding member of Grandma's Marathon and served as its director for 37 years.

I painted houses to make a modest living and, in the fall of 1973, I enrolled at the

University of Minnesota Duluth. I graduated eight years later with a teaching degree.

I coached college and high school cross country running for 18 years.

I was elected to the Duluth City Council and served two four-year terms.

I finally got married at the age of 39 and a half years. Gardening became a passion for me after my wife purchased a wheelbarrow and a shovel.

After retirement, at the age of 60, I started a consulting company to assist nonprofits with their organizational development strategies.

I developed an affection for watching birds, butterflies, dragonflies and bees. I built a 30-foot creek and pond in my backyard to create our own sanctuary. Flower gardens are now everywhere, with fruit trees throughout. Currant and blueberry bushes are present and my colossal rhubarb plant stands tall in the center of everything.

I ran for county commissioner and lost.

I now enjoy spending time with my wife, our eight grandchildren and our precious little great-granddaughter and grandson.

The future is unknown for all of us, but follow your dreams and live your life to the fullest.

Full steam ahead,
Scott Keenan

Made in the USA
Monee, IL
06 August 2024

63311412R00059